Dear Parent:
Your child's love of reading starts here!

Every child learns to read in a different way and at his or her own speed. Some go back and forth between reading levels and read favorite books again and again. Others read through each level in order. You can help your young reader improve and become more confident by encouraging his or her own interests and abilities. From books your child reads with you to the first books he or she reads alone, there are I Can Read Books for every stage of reading:

SHARED READING
Basic language, word repetition, and whimsical illustrations, ideal for sharing with your emergent reader

BEGINNING READING
Short sentences, familiar words, and simple concepts for children eager to read on their own

READING WITH HELP
Engaging stories, longer sentences, and language play for developing readers

READING ALONE
Complex plots, challenging vocabulary, and high-interest topics for the independent reader

ADVANCED READING
Short paragraphs, chapters, and exciting themes for the perfect bridge to chapter books

I Can Read Books have introduced children to the joy of reading since 1957. Featuring award-winning authors and illustrators and a fabulous cast of beloved characters, I Can Read Books set the standard for beginning readers.

A lifetime of discovery begins with the magical words **"I Can Read!"**

Visit www.icanread.com for information
on enriching your child's reading experience.

Marley: The Dog Who Ate My Homework Copyright © 2012 by John Grogan All rights reserved. Manufactured in China. No part of this book may be used or reproduced in any manner whatsoever without written permission except in the case of brief quotations embodied in critical articles and reviews. For information address HarperCollins Children's Books, a division of HarperCollins Publishers, 10 East 53rd Street, New York, NY 10022.
www.icanread.com

Library of Congress catalog card number: 2011940618
ISBN 978-0-06-207481-2 (trade bdg.)—ISBN 978-0-06-207480-5 (pbk.)

12 13 14 15 16   SCP   10 9 8 7 6 5 4 3 2 1   ❖   First Edition

Marley

THE DOG WHO ATE MY HOMEWORK

**BASED ON THE BESTSELLING
BOOKS BY JOHN GROGAN**

COVER ART BY RICHARD COWDREY

TEXT BY CAITLIN BIRCH

**INTERIOR ILLUSTRATIONS BY
RICK WHIPPLE**

HARPER
An Imprint of HarperCollinsPublishers

Marley was waiting
for Cassie to come home.
He'd been waiting all day
to play fetch.

"Not now, Marley," Cassie said.
"I have to work on my project
for school.
I am making a solar system model!"

"The sun is in the middle
of the solar system,"
Cassie said to Mommy.
"Eight planets revolve around
the sun."

Mommy nodded.

"So you need nine round things
for your model," she said.

"What can I use?" Cassie asked.

Just then, Daddy came in
carrying the groceries.
He tossed a grapefruit to Cassie.
"Catch!" Daddy said.

"Woof!"

Marley thought he was finally going to get to play fetch.

"Not now, Marley," Cassie said.

"Daddy just gave me a great idea!"

Soon Cassie had all the fruit

she needed to make her big project.

"I can't wait till tomorrow!"
Cassie said.
"This is the best
solar system model ever."

"And the tastiest," said Daddy.

"Mmm-mmm!" said Baby Louie.

"Great! Now we can play fetch!"
Marley thought.

"Sorry, Marley," Cassie said.
"Now I need to write my report
about the planets and the sun."

Thump!

A noise in the night woke Marley.

Marley got up and crept

into the dining room.

He saw the solar system model.

He watched it gently turning.

Marley poked the big yellow ball
with his nose.

The ball rolled gently.

Marley nosed a red ball.

It spun slowly.

Then Marley sniffed

an orange ball.

Before Marley knew
what he was doing,
one red ball was gone.
He had swallowed it!
Oh no!

"If I take a bite out of this one,"

Marley thought,

"the balls will line up again."

Marley bit one of the orange balls.

It was so sweet!

Soon Marley forgot he was trying

to fix Cassie's project.

Instead, he ate it all up.

In the morning,
Cassie ran downstairs
to pack up her model.
"My solar system is ruined!"
she wailed.
"What am I going to do?"

Marley ran and got his fetch balls.

"Not now, Marley," Daddy said.

"We have to fix Cassie's homework

that you ate!"

"Wait, Daddy," Cassie said.

"Marley's got a great idea!"

Soon Cassie had made
a new solar system.
"This one is even better.
Thanks for your help, Marley!"
she said.

"Oh, Marley," said Cassie.
"My world will always
revolve around you!"